W9-BGW-470

Ethics of Food
Raising Livestock

Patrick Catel

Heinemann Library
Chicago, Illinois

www.heinemannraintree.com
Visit our website to find out more information about Heinemann-Raintree books.

To order:
☎ Phone 888-454-2279
💻 Visit www.heinemannraintree.com to browse our catalog and order online.

Edited by Adam Miller, Andrew Farrow, and Adrian Vigliano
Designed by Ryan Frieson
Illustrated by Mapping Specialists, Ltd. and Planman Technologies
Picture research by Tracy Cummins
Originated by Capstone Global Library Ltd.
Printed and bound in the United States of America by Corporate Graphics in North Mankato, Minnesota
15 14 13 12 11
10 9 8 7 6 5 4 3 2 1

Library of Congress Cataloging-in-Publication Data
Cataloging-in-Publication data is on file at the Library of Congress.

ISBN 978-1-4329-5101-6 (HB)
ISBN 978-1-4329-6191-6 (PB)

Acknowledgements

The author and publisher are grateful to the following for permission to reproduce copyright material: AP Photo p. 34 (West Central Tribune/ Tom Cherveny); Getty Images pp. 17 (Design Pics/ Patrick Swan), 23 (DANIEL GARCIA/AFP), 24 (Digital Vision), 41 (Brian Leatart); istockphoto pp. 9 (© Galina Barskaya), 15 (© Sean Wallentine), 28 (© Carol Gering), 31 (© massimo giovannini); Photolibrary p. 45 (© Trevor Perry); Shutterstock pp. 5 (© clearviewstock), 10 (© Gordon Whyte), 13 (© Ministr-84), 19 (© B Brown), 20 (© ene), 27 (© Dario Sabljak), 29 (© Yarygin), 33 (© Weldon Schloneger), 37 (© Helga Esteb), 39 (© Jose Gil), 43 (© Dani Vincek), 44 (© Dudarev Mikhail), 47 (© Tobik), 48 (© Pieter Janssen).

Cover photograph of newborn chicks being moved on a conveyor belt at a poultry farm in Burgos, northern Spain, 2005 reproduced with permission of Corbis (© FELIX ORDONEZ AUSIN/Reuters).

We would like to thank Christopher Nicolson for his invaluable help in the preparation of this book.

Every effort has been made to contact copyright holders of any material reproduced in this book. Any omissions will be rectified in subsequent printings if notice is given to the publisher.

Contents

Some words are printed in bold, **like this**. You can find out what they mean by looking in the glossary.

Livestock Agriculture: The Animal Farm

Chances are that you are not a livestock farmer, and your family does not live on a farm. In fact, you most likely live in a city or town. However, if you trace your family history back far enough, you probably have family ancestors who were farmers. Many families had a farm sometime in their history, and many kept livestock, which are animals grown on farms for food. Even if your family no longer has anything to do with farming, you are still connected to agriculture every time you shop and eat.

Today, cities and towns around the world are growing as more people move to **urban** areas. In **developed countries** there are now far fewer farmers and farms than there once were—both crop and livestock. However, most of those farms are much larger than farms of the past. As populations have grown, farms have become larger and more efficient in order to provide people with the food they need and want. And many people want meat and dairy—more than ever before.

Impact of the animal farm

The operation of increasingly large livestock farms has allowed more people around the world than ever before to buy the animal products they want. With fast, modern transportation, livestock products from one part of the world can be shipped to almost anywhere else on the globe in order to meet the demand.

So more people around the world can afford and obtain meat and dairy products. But what are the costs of increased livestock production and consumption? How have increased livestock production and consumption affected human health? How have they affected the environment? And finally, there's the consideration of ethics; principles of behavior for deciding what is right and wrong. How do our ideas of right and wrong apply to modern livestock farming? How are the lives of the millions of animals involved in farming affected? How can we act within our sense of what is right and wrong in what we buy and consume? This book will give you the information you need to answer these questions for yourself.

Traditional livestock farms have a variety of animals. They are allowed to roam outside part of the time.

The Rise of Industrial Livestock Farming

Humans naturally desire meat and dairy products because they are rich in protein and other nutrients—as well as flavor. In the distant past, humans only obtained meat by hunting. It could be difficult and dangerous, and people never knew when they might next eat meat. However, the protein-rich animal meat had a lot of calories that could sustain a person for a long time between meals. Every living thing needs to take in energy (in the form of calories) from food in order to survive.

Eventually humans began to farm plants for food. They also began to learn how to keep animals for dairy and food. Sheep were the first to be **domesticated**, or made to work for and live with people, around 9000 BCE. Other animals soon followed. With some effort, the calorie-rich dairy and meat of animals were available to humans without the danger and unpredictability of hunting.

The farm cycle

In **sustainable** agriculture, a farm aims to be continually productive—without harming the environment. Farmers work with the natural surroundings and a variety of species that benefit each other. This is how most farming was less than 100 years ago—and some farmers are returning to this model today, as we will see.

On a sustainable farm, **crop rotation** is used, meaning that different crops are grown in a field each year or season. This ensures that the soil maintains its nutrients. Livestock waste (**manure**) is used as a natural **fertilizer**. The livestock graze on grasses, rotating to different pastures to avoid **overgrazing**. Dried grass is made into bales of hay in the fall, so it can be used for feed in the winter. Chickens provide eggs. Fruit trees provide another source of food and income. Trees also help prevent valuable, nutrient-rich soil from washing away. All of these parts of the traditional farm work in a natural, sustainable cycle.

Less than 100 years ago, small family farms supplied the majority of meat, eggs, and dairy to the world. The family farm formed its own **ecosystem**, with as many as a dozen **species** of plants and animals active at any time (see box at right). Farmers kept a supply of dairy, meat, fruits, and vegetables to meet the needs of their families, plus a little extra to sell to others.

The yearly cycle of a traditional farm made it a self-contained ecosystem.

After humans domesticated animals, they next tried to make them more productive. A farmer may have noticed that a particular cow produced more meat or milk than another cow. So, the farmer could guess that the offspring of that animal might also have the same quality. Therefore, that animal was bred to produce offspring that would also make more meat or milk than others of its kind. This process is called **selective breeding**. Using selective breeding over many years, and with many generations of animals, allowed farmers to produce more food with fewer resources.

The growing demand for meat

Throughout history, meat has played a different role in different cultures. In some areas, such as frozen Arctic areas, meat from hunting and fishing was extremely important, as it was almost the only available food during much of the year. On the other hand, for some cultures meat has often been considered a rare treat. In fact, for much of human history, in many parts of the world, meat was considered a delicacy often reserved for special feasts or holiday meals. Only the very wealthy could eat meat regularly.

But in the second half of the 20th century, people in developed countries had more money to spend. The demand for meat grew, as more people wanted it and could afford it.

ROBERT BAKEWELL

Father of selective breeding

Robert Bakewell (1725–1795) introduced new methods of selective breeding to change the quality of livestock. Bakewell was born in England to a family of farmers. Before taking over the family farm, he traveled around Europe as a young man and learned about other methods of farming. Bakewell is best known for purposely and selectively breeding livestock to produce certain characteristics—such as producing fatter and meatier cattle, or sheep with higher-quality fleece. Some of today's breeds of livestock trace their line back to Bakewell's time. He developed the Leicester sheep, for instance, which produces long wool and a good amount of quality meat. Many of Bakewell's methods were adopted around the world, and are still practiced today.

Demand for meat has continued to increase worldwide ever since, especially with the growing economies of China, India, and other countries. More people with more money means even greater worldwide demand for meat products. Since 1961 the consumption of meat per person has more than doubled worldwide. In **developing countries**, consumption has doubled in just the last 20 years. World meat consumption is expected to double yet again by the year 2050.

The increased demand for meat led to the livestock business becoming **industrialized**, in order to produce enough. This meant creating huge farms, called **factory farms**, that used new machines and technologies to make more agricultural products than ever before. The goal was to produce more meat for more people, while still keeping prices and costs down (and making a profit).

Modern, industrial animal agriculture has made meat cheaper, so that more people are able to enjoy it. Even as little as 100 years ago, meat would have been a treat for most people, not something they could afford to eat every day.

The meat machine

Most corporate livestock farms function like meat factories. Thousands of animals of the same breed live in closed-in **feedlots**. They live among metal buildings, rather than barns. The animals are usually fed from huge **troughs** that mix together different kinds of feed and medicines, with machines regulating the mixture.

Machines in the form of electronic gates and conveyor belts often move animals around. Machines are used in slaughterhouses to quickly kill animals and harvest their meat. Still more machines are used to process nearly every part of every meat animal. The processed meat is then loaded onto more machines (trucks, trains, boats, and airplanes), to be transported around the world.

The trend toward larger farms

Throughout the 20th century, new developments in fields such as technology and machinery made livestock farming—and all farming—easier and much more productive. Increasingly complex machines made processes such as milking cows go more quickly. Just as in 20th-century factories, machines allowed farmers to specialize in particular types of farming. Farms also grew larger, as machines could now work more land more quickly than ever before.

Because of these developments, some small farmers could no longer find ways to effectively compete. Others saw in these changes a chance to make money and sold their land to corporations. Corporations are large companies, or groups of companies, that act together as a single organization. Corporations eventually combined many small farms together to form very large farms.

The worldwide trend in recent years has been to move toward fewer, larger, and more industrialized livestock farms. Industrial farms such as these provide most of the meat products that are consumed in developed countries around the world. However, not all livestock farms are large corporate ones. Many countries still have a wide variety of livestock farms. And, as we will see, some farms have kept, or are returning to, traditional methods (see pages 42 to 45). But the industrial model is still the major one used today.

The international livestock trade

As demand for cheap meat has risen, international trade has grown. In 2006 the total international trade in livestock products amounted to over $237 billion. In 2009 the United States **processed** over 15 percent of the world's total livestock. That year the United States **exported** (sent to other countries) over 5.9 billion kilograms (13 billion pounds) of red meat and **poultry** (birds such as chickens) combined, as well as 242 million cartons of a dozen eggs. Australia, Denmark, France, Germany, the Netherlands, New Zealand, and Brazil are also large exporters of livestock products, including dairy.

Today, the United States alone raises more than 10 billion farmed animals in a single year. That is 10 times the amount raised 70 years ago. Industrial production of livestock is growing more than twice as fast as traditional methods.

The Costs of Industrial Livestock Farming

There are many benefits to industrial livestock farming—and to industrial agriculture in general. Less human labor is needed in industrial agriculture. This keeps costs down, which means food products are cheaper for **consumers**. Faster transportation has meant goods are moved more quickly and easily to market. New techniques in food preservation mean that some foods are available most, if not all, of the year.

Consumers have also benefited from greater variety and availability of goods. More people than ever before enjoy meat, eggs, and dairy—high-calorie, protein-rich foods that were often hard to come by in the past. Livestock farming also provides much-needed jobs. According to the Food and Agriculture Organization of the United Nations (FAO), livestock provides food and income for one billion of the world's poorest people.

Hidden costs of industrialization

At the same time, the world has become increasingly aware that it is paying a price for the move toward industrial livestock farming, including health issues, environmental concerns, and animal welfare issues. These problems have largely been hidden until recently. Whether or not the good ultimately outweighs the bad is a matter of debate.

Health issues

The rise of industrial livestock farming has had some unpleasant side effects on human health. As we have seen, a benefit of meat, eggs, and dairy is that they are rich in protein, which people need to stay healthy. The amount of protein a person requires is continuously studied and depends on many details, including age, weight, overall health, and more. Generally, however, it is estimated that adult men require about 55 grams of protein and adult women require about 45 grams per day.

But the average American consumes around 110 grams of protein a day—about twice what is recommended. About 75 grams of that comes from animals. This has led large numbers of people around the world to an increase in heart disease, some types of cancer, and diabetes, a serious disease in which there is too much sugar in the blood.

The desire to get a lot of calories for as little money as possible encourages some people to eat unhealthy foods.

There are many sources of protein, and people do not have to get it from meat in order to have enough and be healthy. According to the Harvard School of Public Health, vegetable sources of protein are excellent choices, and the best animal protein choices are fish and poultry. But because factory farms have made meat and animal products cheap and readily available—and often more affordable than fresh produce—many people eat too many of these foods (see box at right).

The cost of a healthy diet

We live in a fast-paced world, and people often need a quick meal. People also try to save money. Fast food (such as a burger with fries) provides what many people want, with fast, cheap, and delicious (to some) meals. Unfortunately, fast-food meals are usually not very nutritious. Fresh fruits and vegetables are considered the healthiest of foods. However, the cost of fruits and vegetables has risen more quickly than the cost of a fast-food hamburger. The economic situation of the modern food industry does not always encourage good health.

Antibiotics and chemicals

Eating too much meat is not the only health concern posed by the rising popularity of industrial livestock farming. Many people are also concerned about potentially harmful substances that the industrial process adds to meat and animal products.

For example, on industrial farms, most livestock are fed large amounts of **antibiotics** in small, daily doses. This is done to help keep them alive in the stressful and unhealthy situations in which they live, and also to fatten them up (see pages 20 to 35). It is also because antibiotics help animals such as cows process an unnatural diet of corn (see box at right).

However, the constant use of antibiotics creates infectious germs, called pathogens, such as *E.Coli* and salmonella. If humans are exposed to pathogens found in meat, they can catch diseases. But when these people seek treatment, the antibiotics normally prescribed—the same ones used on livestock—are not always effective against the pathogens. This is because the pathogens have already built up resistance to antibiotics in the animals.

Mad cow disease

There are other ways livestock can pass disease on to humans. In the past, some cattle farms fed processed cow parts from slaughterhouses back to feedlots to be used as feed for other cows. Even though cattle are herbivores (plant eaters) by nature, this was the most efficient way for the industry to get the cattle their required protein.

Scientists figured out that this practice was spreading bovine spongiform encephalopathy (BSE), also known as mad cow disease. The first cases of mad cow disease were discovered in British cattle in 1986, but the disease was soon discovered elsewhere. If humans eat this infected meat, they can develop a fatal brain disease called Creutzfeldt-Jakob disease (CJD).

Even though cows are no longer fed processed cow, in some places they are still fed animal proteins in the form of processed chicken, fish, and pig. Some health experts worry that these practices could cause similar problems in the future.

Cattle in the United States are also given **hormones** such as growth hormones. Hormones are chemical substances produced in the bodies of living things that influence a body's growth and condition. Giving cattle extra growth hormones allows the cows to grow larger more quickly, which means more profit for the business. However, there is evidence that the hormones given to cattle are passed on to the human consumer, which may lead to human health problems. The European Union banned the import of U.S. hormone-fed cattle out of human health concerns.

These cows are eating feed on a farm in Minnesota. After widespread concerns about mad cow disease, new regulations were put in place to ensure that cattle are no longer fed processed cow.

Fighting nature: Making cattle eat corn

In the U.S., a modern industrial cattle farm can have tens of thousands of cattle packed onto a feedlot. As many as a million pounds of feed corn pass through these farms each day. There are also thousands of gallons of liquid fat and protein supplements, as well as large vats of antibiotics.

Large cattle farms feed corn to cattle because it helps them get fat quickly, so that their meat can be harvested. Corn-fed cows also develop a higher proportion of body fat than they would on a natural diet. The other major reason corn is used in most industrial feedlots is simple economics. Due to modern farming technologies, corn has become extremely cheap to produce in huge quantities.

So, what's wrong with feeding corn to cattle? The problem is that **ruminants** like cattle are not adapted to eat corn—their natural diet is grass. Ruminants are hoofed mammals such as cattle, sheep, and goats that have a stomach divided into four compartments—one of which is called the rumen. The rumen can digest grass, turning it into a nutritious protein.

The only way to make cattle eat corn is to feed them medicines that shut down their rumens. For this reason, most of the health problems feedlot cattle experience can be traced back to their diet. Soy is another grain used as cattle feed, especially in the United Kingdom. But soy creates similar problems and results when it is fed to cattle.

Environmental concerns

Beyond human health, many people worry about what industrial agriculture does to the environment.

Soil: A nonrenewable resource

A resource is something that can be used by people. A nonrenewable resource is one that cannot be replaced once it is used. Soil is considered nonrenewable because it forms so slowly. It can take hundreds of years for a few inches of soil to form. Some of the best soil found today may have taken thousands of years to develop. Worldwide, through a process called erosion, soil is being washed away 10 to 40 times faster than it is being replaced. That means that cropland the size of the state of Indiana is being destroyed each year. But what leads to these levels of erosion?

Livestock such as beef and dairy cattle eat grass. However, overgrazing can lead to bare and compacted soil—which leads to erosion. To prevent this, some farmers develop grazing plans that aim to rotate the animals among different pastures. That way, no individual pastures are overgrazed. This maintains the richness of the soil, and the grass continually grows back. Crop rotation also helps the problem. Hedgerows and stone walls found around farms in the United Kingdom and parts of Europe serve the same purpose. Still, the loss of soil continues to be a problem.

Deforestation

Converting more land for livestock development contributes to deforestation, or loss of forests, in some countries. Valuable forests have been cleared in Central and South America to create animal pastures, which has destroyed valuable ecosystems.

Manure lagoons

On large feedlots, it is not uncommon for packed-together animals to be constantly living in a mixture of manure and mud or dust. In large livestock operations, the manure is often kept in lagoons (shallow, artificial ponds). Some of this manure is sprayed over fields, which may not be able to absorb it all as fertilizer. Some of it may end up leaking into local water supplies. Gases from manure lagoons also cause damaging rain, called acid rain, and air pollution.

There has also been an increasing concentration of livestock production in single locations. These local areas cannot absorb all the animal manure, and it becomes a waste product, rather than a resource.

What would you do?

The best use of resources?

The FAO estimates that 30 percent of Earth's ice-free land is involved in livestock production.

Some people argue that livestock farming uses too many of the planet's resources for the amount of food it produces. More livestock means more feed is needed for the animals, which means more cropland is devoted to crops for farm animals. People argue that, due to the world's growing population, land good for growing crops should instead be used for grains, such as rice, that can feed more people using a smaller amount of resources.

The FAO points out that the relationship between demand for animal feed and creating enough food for humans is more complex than that. If there were no animals consuming surplus (extra) grain, it would probably not be produced to begin with—rather than going to those around the world who need it. Also, many areas of the world dedicated to pasture for livestock would be too dry or cold to support crops. What do you think? Is the land used in livestock production being used wisely?

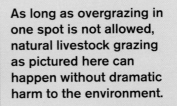

As long as overgrazing in one spot is not allowed, natural livestock grazing as pictured here can happen without dramatic harm to the environment.

Industrial livestock products and fossil fuels

One of the major environmental concerns today is **global warming**. This is a general increase in world temperatures caused by increased amounts of **greenhouse gases** around the Earth. Greenhouse gases such as carbon dioxide and methane trap heat above the Earth, raising its temperature—similar to the glass ceiling of a greenhouse. The burning of **fossil fuels** releases greenhouse gases and adds to global warming. The FAO estimates that livestock production generates almost one-fifth (18 percent) of the world's greenhouse gases.

Farmers must use a lot of fertilizer to create feed crops like corn. Among other things, fertilizers contain nitrogen, phosphorus, and potassium, which plants need to grow. However, the processes used to make these fertilizers require fuel for heat in chemical reactions. The fuels used are usually fossil fuels, such as oil, because they are cheap and easily attained. For this reason, the production of fertilizer uses up a lot of fossil fuel. The FAO estimates that the production of fertilizer for feed crops may be responsible for 41 million tonnes (45.2 million tons) of carbon dioxide per year worldwide. Carbon dioxide is considered the greenhouse gas with the most potential to cause global warming.

One of the key resources that makes all the machines and chemicals work in modern livestock agriculture is the fossil fuel petroleum. Oil (from petroleum) is needed to run feedlots, slaughterhouses, and egg and dairy machines. It takes additional oil to transport livestock products across countries and the world in the growing international trade. The fossil fuels used to run the machines of factory farming cause over 90 million tonnes (99.2 million tons) of carbon dioxide emissions worldwide each year. Processing, packaging, and transportation account for millions more tons of carbon dioxide each year.

The FAO estimates that livestock themselves are responsible for a higher share of greenhouse gases than transportation. This is because industrial animal agriculture produces methane, a greenhouse gas that can contribute to global warming. Methane occurs naturally as a gas released from animal manure. Huge livestock farms create huge amounts of manure, often collected in the manure lagoons mentioned on page 16. This creates a more concentrated release of methane into the air. Nitrous oxide is another greenhouse gas released from animal manure, and in larger quantities from manure lagoons.

Environment watch

Fertilizer, herbicides, and pesticides

Farmers often use artificial fertilizers to take the place of animal manure and replenish nutrients in the soil. **Herbicides** are also used to kill unwanted weeds that compete with crops. **Pesticides** are used to kill unwanted pests that would eat crops. Fertilizers, herbicides, and pesticides make farms more productive. However, the chemicals used in these products can have negative, unpredicted consequences.

Excess amounts of these chemicals run off of the land during heavy rains and wash into rivers, lakes, and other freshwater supplies. This can hurt the environment and damage people's drinking water. Small amounts of the chemicals are sometimes found on the farmed foods themselves. Since those grains are fed to livestock, they consume some of the chemicals as well. Since artificial fertilizers take the place of animal manure, there is the added problem of what to do with all the unused poop! That becomes another environmental concern.

Machinery and chemical science have made it easy to quickly spray a large field of crops with pesticides. But what are the consequences for people who eat products from animals raised on these crops?

The Lives of Livestock

In addition to the issues of human health and the environment, there is, of course, the issue of how the animals themselves are affected by industrial livestock farming.

Most people like to believe livestock lead decent lives, free from suffering, until they are killed to provide food. Unfortunately, the feelings and quality of life of livestock are not the major concern of industrial animal agriculture. Instead, the system is geared toward efficiency and profit. Animals are bred to grow as large as possible extremely quickly—so that more meat can be harvested. They often live in overcrowded conditions and are not free to roam, graze, or follow their instincts, or natural tendencies.

Knowing where our food comes from

In order to understand where the majority of meat, eggs, and dairy we buy comes from, we must trace these foods back to their animal origins. By knowing what most farm animals' lives are like, we can know where our livestock products come from and what it takes to get them to our tables as life-sustaining food.

Of course, there are a variety of farms around the world. The lives of the animals discussed in this chapter represent the typical lives of the majority of animals farmed for food in developed countries. Other methods of farming animals for food are discussed on pages 42 to 45.

Thousands of turkeys stand crowded in this feed house in California, less than a week before each one will be part of a Thanksgiving feast somewhere in the United States.

Extreme breeding

Livestock animals have become extremely productive, especially over the last 60 years or so. Meat animals now grow bigger and faster than ever, dairy cows produce much more milk, and hens lay many more eggs. For example:

- In 1950 the average dairy cow on a traditional U.S. farm produced about 2,520 liters (665 gallons) of milk per year. By 2002 the typical cow at an industrial dairy farm produced about 8,780 liters (2,320 gallons) of milk per year—a 240 percent increase!

- Today's pigs grow to about 120 kilograms (260 pounds) in a little less than six months, which is 18 kilograms (40 pounds) more than the average six-month-old pig weighed in 1950.

- By 2000 chickens required only 47 days to reach slaughter weight—which was 23 fewer days than in 1950. The 47-day-old chicken of today is also two-thirds bigger than a 70-day-old chicken from 1950.

The extreme productivity of modern livestock has driven down the cost of animal products. However, the animals themselves have suffered as a result of selective breeding efforts. For example, broiler chickens (chickens raised for meat) have very fast metabolisms, which is the body process that changes food into energy. Their fast metabolisms allow them to grow more quickly, which means that meat gets to the market more quickly. However, the fast metabolisms of broiler chickens can also cause them to suffer heart or lung failure. Pigs are bred so large that they commonly suffer from foot and joint problems. Dairy cows produce so much milk that they suffer from infections and other health problems. Do you think the extra productivity of modern livestock is worth the problems it causes for the animals?

The life of a meat cow

The word "cow" is often used to describe a mature male or female bovine, but males are also called steers. To produce a meat steer, a female cow is **artificially inseminated**, meaning it is made pregnant with scientific equipment. Scientists choose the father based on the quality of the meat it produces.

A steer is born on a ranch that is usually still a family-owned operation or small business. The calf (baby cow) is given a number, just like its mother. This helps the ranch keep track of the animals. As soon as the calf can stand on its own and nurse from its mother, they are both sent out on grassy pasture.

The calf spends the next six months with its mother, grazing on grasses at the ranch, as beef steers have done for hundreds of years. The most difficult part of these six months is when the steer is branded (burned with a mark) and **castrated** (has its testicles removed in order to reduce aggressiveness and prevent unwanted breeding).

After six months, the calf is **weaned** from its mother. Weaning is the process of getting a young animal used to food other than its mother's milk. The calf is taken away, and the mother cow is distressed to find the calf gone, often crying out for hours. Weaning is a stressful time of change for a calf, and it is more likely to get sick. Weaning is important for ranchers, however, in order to free mother cows to have more calves. It also prepares the calf for its next stage of life.

The calf is between about 230 and 270 kilograms (500 and 600 pounds) when it is rounded up with other calves into a pen. Here the calves are confined and taught to eat from a trough. Their diet now changes from grass to grains such as corn or soy. For two months or so, the calves' bodies are forced to adjust to eating grains, an unnatural diet for them (see page 15). They are fed antibiotics to allow their bodies to process the grains. The confinement and diet during this time help to prepare calves for the rest of their lives on the feedlot.

Life on a corporate feedlot is crowded, dirty, and smelly. The steer will live out the rest of its life here, for a total lifespan of about 14 to 16 months. It will then be taken to the slaughterhouse, usually nearby. There it is killed quickly, usually with a bolt gun, a kind of gun that strikes an animal brain dead, so that it does not suffer. The steer is then hung up and its throat is cut, to allow the blood to drain out. It is then processed, and almost every part of the animal is used.

The early life of a dairy cow

The Holstein is a black-and-white breed of cow that originated in Europe. The Holstein is known for its milk production. It is by far the most popular breed in dairy farming. A Holstein calf usually weighs between 40 and 45 kilograms (90 and 100 pounds) at birth. If it is a female calf, it will stay on the dairy farm and be raised to eventually produce milk, like its mother. What happens to male calves is another story.

The dairy calf is normally weaned within two to three days of birth. After those first two to three days, the calf is taken away. That way, the mother cow's milk can be processed for sale. The calf is then fed a high-protein formula, usually made from animal products gathered from slaughterhouses. The calf is first fed grain at around 7 to 10 days old.

Beef cattle are not allowed to fulfill their natural instincts on an industrial farm. These cattle are being unloaded from a truck at a meat processing plant.

A heifer is a young female cow that has not yet given birth to a calf. At six months old the heifer is usually fed grain and hay, but it may also be allowed to graze in a pasture, eating grass. This depends on the price of feed and the practices of the individual dairy farm. The Holstein heifer weighs about 180 kilograms (400 pounds) at this age. The goal of the dairy farmer is to have the heifer gain about 0.8 kilograms (1.75 pounds) each day.

Dairy technology

Dairy farms use modern technology to be as efficient as possible. Larger farms often use a rotating milking parlor. This is a large, round platform with milking stalls for cows all around the edge (see photo below). The dairy cows enter and are milked, and sometimes fed, as the platform slowly rotates. Each cow leaves when it is finished being milked after a full rotation, with another cow moving in to take its place. The process continues with cows constantly coming and going, usually 24 hours a day, so that milk is always being produced.

After a year the heifer is called a yearling and weighs about 320 kilograms (700 pounds). After another year the cow weighs about 545 kilograms (1,200 pounds) and is ready to have its first calf.

The adult life of a dairy cow

From the age of two, the cow will be artificially inseminated to produce a calf every 12 to 14 months, just as its mother did. It will produce milk for the farm after each calf is born, and it will continue to grow. At about five years old, the mature dairy cow weighs over 680 kilograms (1,500 pounds), has already had three or four calves, and can produce over 45 liters (12 gallons) of milk a day after having a calf.

The lifespan of a dairy cow can be up to 25 years. However, few adult dairy cows are kept longer than five years. Most likely the dairy cow's milk production will fall after five years. At that point it no longer makes economic sense to feed the cow, and it is then sold for slaughter.

Meat from dairy cows

When you buy hamburger at the supermarket or order a fast-food burger, there is a good chance you are getting meat from a dairy cow, rather than a meat cow. Female dairy cows that are no longer productive are also slaughtered for meat. Since they were bred to produce milk, the meat is poorer quality. For that reason, adult dairy cows are usually processed into ground beef.

Because dairy cows only produce milk after having a calf, dairy farms produce many calves, about half of which are males. A male calf will never produce milk, so it is not valuable to the dairy farmer. So, the male calves are sold for meat. Some end up as veal (calf meat). Calves raised for veal are often isolated in crates as they grow and completely deprived of the ability to fulfill their instincts. The cruelty endured by most calves to make veal has become well known since the 1980s. As a result, veal has become less popular, and some veal farms have changed their practices.

The life of a farm pig

Pigs are domesticated swine. They are also called hogs. Pigs are generally considered to be as intelligent as dogs—maybe even smarter (see the box on page 27). They are increasingly raised on industrial hog farms, which are replacing traditional, family-run farms.

Sows (female adult pigs) give birth to eight piglets on average. A piglet born at an industrial farm is weaned from its mother about 10 days after birth. This is stressful for the mother sow and the piglet. In nature the piglet would normally stay close and drink its mother's milk for 13 weeks.

The piglet is taken off its mother's milk and given feed that includes hormones so that it will gain weight more quickly than it would naturally. The piglet is castrated if it is a male.

Sometimes the piglet's corkscrew tail is cut off and its ears and sharper teeth are clipped, to prevent pigs from biting each other in crammed pens. These procedures are usually done without anesthetic (painkiller), using a pair of pliers, steel clippers, or similar tools.

The piglet is bottle-fed by machines until it reaches around 25 kilograms (55 pounds). At that point it is moved to begin its life with the rest of the pig population.

The pig will spend the rest of its life crowded together with thousands of other pigs, barely able to move, confined indoors in a large building. In this unnatural, crowded environment, the pigs are not allowed to follow their natural habits and instincts.

The confinement buildings for pigs are often hundreds of feet long. They have slatted floors, which are floors with space in between beams. This allows manure and urine to fall into pits below. The crowded conditions and stress lead to fighting among the pigs, including biting. This is the reason the pigs' tails, teeth, and ears are clipped—to prevent the stressed, angry pigs from biting easy-to-reach areas on other pigs such as tails and ears, and the infections this can cause.

The pig will reach about 115 kilograms (250 pounds) at about four to six months old. It will then be slaughtered for meat. Breeding sows are sent to slaughter when they are about two to three years old—and when they can no longer produce piglets, as the factory farm wants them to.

> "The pig is . . . the most abused of all our farm animals. We can say this partly because of all of them it is certainly the most intelligent and gregarious [friendly]."
> —Hugh Fearnley-Whittingstall, celebrity chef and author

Small pig farms such as this one, where pigs have even a small amount of space to move around in, exist as a minority in the pork industry.

What do you think?

That's one smart pig!

Domesticated pigs are very smart. They will even work together to move latches and open the gates to their pen. According to Ken Kephart, a professor of animal science, "The smartest swine even open up the rest of the pens to let the others out." Not only are pigs quite smart, they are also friendly. Does knowing how smart domesticated pigs can be change your feelings about eating pork products?

The many uses of farm pigs

Besides the many meat products that come from pigs, various parts of the pig are also used in other products and industrial processes. You might be surprised to know which items are sometimes made using pigs. Here is a sample of products and the pig parts that are sometimes used in their production:

body lotion
  fatty acids

bullets
  bone gelatin

bread
  protein from hair

chewing gum
  gelatin

cigarettes
  hemoglobin from blood

cosmetics
  fatty acids, collagen

crayons
  fatty acids

fabric softener
  fatty acids

fertilizer
  processed hair

fruit juice
  gelatin

medicinal pills
  gelatin

paints
  fatty acids

paint brushes
  hair

photographic film
  bone gelatin

paper
  bone gelatin

shoes
  bone glue

tambourines
  bladder

toothpaste
  glycerine from bone fat

train brakes
  bone ash

yogurt
  bone calcium

The life of a farm sheep or goat

Sheep and goats are raised for meat and milk. Some breeds of sheep are raised for their thick, woolly fur. Certain goats, such as the Angora and Cashmere, are also raised for their wool. In North America, Europe, Great Britain, and China, domesticated goats are raised mostly for their milk, which is used to make cheese.

A young sheep is called a lamb, as is its meat. Meat from an older sheep is called mutton. Sheep farming is practiced all over the world, but New Zealand and Australia are well known for sheep production. Their abundant pastureland and mild winter weather are good for sheep, which are a big part of the culture and economy in those countries. Sheep and goats are ruminants, like cattle (see page 15).

Intensive farming, meaning farming that creates a lot of food from a small amount of land, is much less common with sheep and goats. They usually spend a great deal of time grazing outdoors. There is still very little factory farming of sheep, and no factory goat farming.

Goats and sheep are more likely than other livestock to be raised in a traditional manner and allowed to range free and graze, following their natural behavior and instincts.

The life of a broiler chicken

Broiler chickens are chickens raised for meat, rather than for laying eggs. Almost all chicken meat you buy and eat—including from supermarkets, restaurants, and even your school cafeteria—is produced by intensive factory farming, unless the packaging specifically says otherwise.

A chick is first **incubated** (kept warm until hatching) at a large hatchery. The egg sits on a shelf with thousands of others, with machines automatically rotating them. The chick hatches after 21 days or so, along with the others. The chicks then go to a growing facility called a broiler house. The broiler house grows as many as 10,000 to 30,000 chickens in a single shed. They are given feed that includes antibiotics and drugs to increase their appetites. The goal is to fatten them up as quickly as possible at the lowest possible cost.

At this point it would be difficult to keep track of a single chicken. As the chickens grow, conditions get more and more crowded. Because of the crowding and stress, tens or even hundreds of chickens suffocate, are crushed, or contract diseases. Chickens that become aggressive have the ends of their beaks clipped to avoid injuries (see page 32).

Because they are the products of selective breeding, it takes only six weeks for the chickens to weigh enough (about 1.4 to 2.3 kilograms, or 3 to 5 pounds) to be slaughtered. That means the life of a broiler chicken is eight weeks total. The chickens are crowded into crates and taken to the slaughterhouse, where they are electrically stunned before being killed. Once the crop of thousands of chickens is sent to slaughter, the shed is then cleaned for the next group.

What is "free range"?

When you are at the supermarket, you may see the term "**free range**" on packaging to describe a method of livestock farming, especially with chicken. This term means that the animals are allowed to roam freely, rather than being caged or contained indoors.

In the United States, however, a farm can easily claim to be "free range." U.S. Department of Agriculture (USDA) regulations do not say what the outside range needs to be like, or the amount of time an animal must have access to it. Even just having an open door to the outside, regardless of whether any of the chickens actually use it (or even know it is there), can allow a producer to label its chicken meat as "free range."

Many broiler chickens raised on factory farms suffer from poor health because of the extremely crowded and dirty conditions.

The life of a laying chicken

A laying chicken is a hen (female chicken) that produces eggs. As with meat, most eggs are produced on factory farms. Laying chickens are bred to produce more eggs. Thousands of them are incubated and hatched at large hatcheries, much like broiler chickens.

The thousands of baby chicks are then moved along a conveyor belt, where workers determine if they are male or female (as seen in the cover photo of this book). Since the male chicks will not lay eggs, they are not considered to be valuable and are killed or allowed to die at birth—often through suffocation or by being ground up using industrial grinding machines.

At about 21 weeks old and 1.4 kilograms (3 pounds) in weight, the chicken is moved into a laying house. It will now live with up to 10 other laying hens in a cage no bigger than 1.5 by 1.5 meters (5 by 5 feet) in size. Its cage is one of many stacked four to six high and in rows inside a large building.

The hen will produce between 250 and 300 eggs in a year. Most laying houses are automated, with a constant supply of feed and water provided to each cage. The cages are tilted slightly to one side, and conveyor belts collect the eggs as they roll down. The eggs then move to a room where they are cleaned, sorted, and packaged.

Laying chickens are more aggressive than broiler chickens by nature, and so they usually have their beaks clipped to prevent injury (see box at right). Most laying hens are no longer productive after about two years.

Debeaking and forced molting

Debeaking is when a chicken has the end of its beak clipped, so it cannot injure another bird. There is evidence that this is painful for the bird, especially if too much of the beak is clipped off.

Forced molting of laying chickens is another practice that many feel is cruel. Molting is when a bird loses its feathers. This happens naturally, and the bird cannot produce eggs during those months. Without the natural, shorter daylight in autumn as a trigger, laying hens kept indoors will not molt. This will decrease the production and quality of their eggs. Forced molting increases the birds' productivity and egg quality, so the laying house loses less time and fewer eggs (and therefore less money). To force a laying chicken to molt, all feed is removed until it loses between 25 and 35 percent of its body weight. One of the side effects is that the chicken's bones become fragile and often break. The process also makes the hens more susceptible to diseases, such as salmonella, which can be passed on in their eggs.

At that point the chicken is of little value to the company. It is sold cheaply and used to provide meat for processed foods, such as canned chicken soup and pet food. If no money is likely to be made, the chicken is simply killed and discarded.

Case study:
The European Union stops the use of battery cages

The tiny cages laying hens are often kept in are called battery cages. The battery cages usually only provide space the size of a letter-sized sheet of paper for the hen. It cannot move or even spread its wings. The European Union has decided this is a cruel practice, and battery cages will no longer be allowed there after January 1, 2012.

When looking for meat and eggs in the market, you may encounter the term "cage-free." "Cage-free" means that the hens that laid the eggs were not kept in battery cages, although it doesn't necessarily mean that the hens lived on a farm with access to the outdoors, such as the one pictured here.

The life of a farm turkey

Many factory farms raise turkeys as well as chickens. The life of a turkey is very similar to the life of a broiler chicken, but turkeys live longer and produce more meat. Both male and female turkeys are raised and processed for their meat. Since turkeys live longer than chickens, most broiler houses keep three separate flocks at different stages of growth.

The turkey will be raised four to five months before slaughter. Until that time it will live in conditions very similar to a factory-farmed broiler chicken. As with broiler chickens, an aggressive turkey will have its beak clipped to prevent injuries in the crowded shed.

> "The industrial birds have been bred in such a way that they can't really survive in nature—they [turkeys] can't even mate. . . . Both turkeys and chickens have really lost their ability to live. They can't even walk very well—their bodies are just not sound."
> —Frank Reese, farmer, Good Shepherd Turkey Ranch (a natural, free-range turkey farm)

Some free-range farms now specialize in "heritage" breeds of turkey, which look very different from turkeys raised on industrial farms (see page 20).

The turkey has been bred to grow large very quickly. It has also been bred to produce large breasts, in order to meet consumer demand for turkey breast meat. These characteristics make it so that the turkey cannot reproduce naturally, and may even have trouble standing.

The life of a farm duck or goose

Both male and female ducks and geese are raised for food. As demand for duck meat and goose down (their soft, fluffy layer of feathers) has grown, so has the factory farming of these birds. Ducks are more likely to be raised on a factory farm than geese. Many geese are still raised on small farms as free-range birds.

When a duck or goose is factory farmed, it may never see the outdoors or sunlight. It is raised in a fashion similar to a broiler chicken or turkey. This means the bird is raised in a crowded, dirty shed along with hundreds or thousands of others. There is little concern for the normal instincts and behaviors of the bird. In nature, ducks normally spend 80 percent of their time on water. However, they are only allowed dripping water to drink in the factory farm shed.

Many birds are unhealthy from disease, and some die. Because of the conditions and stress, the birds sometimes pull out their own feathers. Some farmers cut the upper bill of the duck or goose to prevent this, since goose down and duck feathers are valuable as filler for pillows and other items.

Foie gras

Foie gras (pronounced "fwah grah") is a food made from the liver of a duck or goose that has been specially fattened. It is considered a rich delicacy. Usually foie gras is produced by force-feeding the duck or goose, in order to fatten its liver. This is done using a feeding tube to force the food into the bird's esophagus. The tube food passes down from the mouth to the stomach. With modern pumps, this usually takes about two to three seconds.

Many people consider the practice cruel, and some places have banned the use of force-feeding to produce foie gras. Because of this, some farms have adopted a new way of raising geese and ducks for foie gras. The birds are fed or allowed to graze without force-feeding. They are then slaughtered at the time when their livers are naturally fattened before they migrate (travel to another part of the world) in the winter.

Do Livestock Have Rights?

If you are a meat eater, perhaps you are rethinking your meal choices after reading about how the average farm animal lives on an industrial farm. Or maybe you are not. Some people feel that animals raised for meat, eggs, and dairy sacrifice their rights for the greater good of providing humans with food.

But most people would agree, when asked, that cruelty to animals is wrong. Most people would also agree that even food animals should not be treated cruelly during the time that they are alive.

Cruelty to livestock

As we have seen, there is evidence that animals raised for food using industrial farming methods do indeed suffer. Sometimes it is when beef cattle and other ruminants are forced to eat surplus (extra) grains such as corn and soy against their nature. Sometimes it is from stresses such as crowded conditions, being constantly pregnant, or having young taken from them. And sometimes it is from procedures that have been proven painful, such as clipping birds' beaks or pigs' tails. Many animals live in a constant state of ill health. They are unable to satisfy their instincts and natural behaviors.

How does intensive animal farming affect me?

Many of the cruelest practices found in animal agriculture result from the desire to keep prices down. For example, some animals, such as baby male chicks in laying operations, are simply discarded and left to die or immediately killed because they are not worth the cost to keep alive.

As a consumer, you will pay less for food if steps like this are taken to save money. But do you feel this sort of cruelty is worth the savings? How much more would you pay to know that the animals your food came from were treated well and lived natural lives?

TEMPLE GRANDIN

Reducing animal stress

Temple Grandin is a doctor of animal science, professor, and author. She also suffers from autism, a mental disorder that makes it difficult for a person to respond to and communicate with other people. Grandin's autism gives her the unique ability to perceive the slightest details. This gives her insight into the minds of animals.

Her ability to understand animals has led Grandin to be able to design more **humane** methods and equipment for handling animals in the livestock industry. She has designed facilities located in the United States, Europe, New Zealand, Canada, Australia, Mexico, and other countries. Grandin's designs for systems and devices, and her writings about animal behavior, have helped reduce stress on livestock around the world during their handling. Today, Grandin teaches courses on livestock behavior and facility design at Colorado State University and works with the livestock industry on facility design, livestock handling, and animal welfare.

Temple Grandin, shown here at the premier of a film about her life.

The case for animal rights

Some people argue that animals should have the same rights as humans. They make several arguments to support this point of view, such as:

- Animals are similar in biological complexity to humans.

- Animals are conscious and know what is happening to them.

- Animals prefer some things and dislike others, and they make choices.

- Animals try to live in a way that gives them the best quality of life and the most comfort. The quality and length of life matter to animals.

Many people throughout history have made these arguments. Both religious people and those who do not follow specific religious teachings have argued that harming animals in any way is simply a wrong, evil practice. The following is a sample of these ideas:

> "The question is not, Can they reason?, nor Can they talk?, but, Can they suffer?"
> —English philosopher Jeremy Bentham

> "We can judge the heart of a man by his treatment of animals."
> —German philosopher Immanuel Kant

> "If a man aspires towards [aims for] a righteous life, his first act of abstinence [avoidance] is from injury to animals."
> —Russian writer Leo Tolstoy

> "Until we stop harming all other living beings, we are still savages."
> —U.S. inventor Thomas Edison

> "The worst sin towards our fellow creatures is not to hate them, but to be indifferent to them, that's the essence of inhumanity."
> —Irish playwright George Bernard Shaw

> "The greatness of a nation and its moral progress can be judged by the way its animals are treated."
> —Indian leader Mohandas Gandhi

The case against animal rights

Of course, a number of arguments are made against animals having the same rights as humans, such as:

- Animals do not think and are not really conscious in the same way that humans are.

- Animals do not have souls and were put on the planet to serve human beings. (This is a religious argument that some people make.)

- Animals do not behave morally (with a sense of right and wrong), and are therefore not part of the same moral category as human beings.

- Animals act on instinct, not thought—and especially not moral thought.

Those who believe animals do not have rights finally ask why human beings should have obligations toward animals if animals do not have obligations to other animals or to human beings. Those against equal rights for animals also ask where it would stop. The logic of equal rights for different creatures could grow to mean that even the simplest plants and animals have rights equal to human beings, to the point where there is no longer common sense in human society.

"The animal rights movement illustrates the. . . nature of a moral passion become immoral by virtue of its extremism. In the name of the laudable [admirable] quality of humaneness, the use of animals for food, clothing and medical experimentation is prohibited. Research that could save your child's life, or save you from an excruciating disease, is declared **unethical**. The result is inhumanity toward man."
—Charles Griswold, professor of philosophy at Boston University

"If all animals had a right to freedom to live their lives without molestation, then someone would have to protect them from one another. But this is absurd…"
—Mary Warnock, *An Intelligent Person's Guide to Ethics*

These protesters are defending the use of animals in medical research for humans.

Making Choices

Industrial farming has helped feed the world and has given even the poorest people the chance to eat meat. Few would argue that the life of an animal is more valuable than the life of a human.

People also want their money to go as far as possible, and they are always looking for a bargain at the supermarket. The agricultural industry is producing the foods people want at the prices they want to pay.

However, after reading about how livestock are often raised, you may think that the livestock industry is cruel. You may also have concerns about the damage it can cause to human health and the environment.

But most people are not aware of the details of how all of their food is raised. They are not aware of exactly how their supermarket meat, eggs, and dairy are produced, or how the farm animals behind those products live. As people become more informed, they realize there are different choices they can make.

Vegetarians and vegans

Some people make the choice not to eat meat at all. People who feel it is not morally right to eat animals often choose to become vegetarian or vegan. Vegetarians eat fruits, vegetables, grains, and nuts, but no meat. There are several types of vegetarianism. Some vegetarians eat eggs and dairy products. Vegans are stricter, refusing to eat, or use, any animal product, including clothing such as leather that is made from animals.

Vegetarian protein options
Legumes (such as beans and peas)
Nuts and seeds
Dairy products (if not vegan)
Cereals and grains (such as bread)
Algae
Soya beans (such as tofu)
Seitan
Mushrooms
Quorn (made from egg white and mushroom-like fungus)

There are many high-protein options for people who choose not to eat meat.

"Nothing will benefit human health and increase chances for survival of life on Earth as much as the evolution to a vegetarian diet."
—German-U.S. scientist Albert Einstein (1879–1955)

With plenty of vegetarian options to provide similar protein and nutrients (see chart below), vegetarians point out that eating meat is not necessary for good health. In fact, eating less meat can benefit a person's health.

Kosher and halal

Certain religions also address the issue of whether it is spiritually right to eat certain animals and animal products. "Kosher" describes what is fit and proper to eat for those of the Jewish faith. "Halal" describes what is fit and proper to eat for those of the Muslim faith. In both cases, no meat from pigs is allowed. The mixing of meat and dairy, including any utensils used with them, is also forbidden.

For meat to be kosher or halal, the animal must be slaughtered in a particular way. This is done with a quick, clean cut of the throat with a sharp blade. This is considered a painless and humane method of slaughter. It also allows for the quick and complete draining of the blood, which is another requirement. For meat to be kosher, the person who performs the slaughter, called a *shochet*, must be trained in Jewish law. Muslims are allowed to eat meat properly slaughtered by people of Jewish and Christian faith. However, halal requires that a prayer to Allah (God) be said before slaughtering.

The growth of alternative agriculture

For those people who want to eat meat, many are increasingly asking for more options. In the 1990s, people became more aware of the specific practices of industrial animal farming. Many were upset about the treatment of animals—not to mention the chemicals, hormones, and antibiotics used in crop and livestock agriculture. As a result, they sought out food that had been raised more naturally. People were looking for an alternative to industrial farming, and so "alternative agriculture" grew in popularity. "Alternative agriculture" was crop and livestock farming that was done in a more natural and sustainable way.

SIR ALBERT HOWARD

Sir Albert Howard (1873–1947) was an English agronomist. Agronomy is the science of soil management and the production of crops. Howard wrote *An Agricultural Testament* in 1940. The book's ideas strongly influenced the principles of organic agriculture and the organic movement. Although he never used the term "**organic**," Howard spoke of the idea that all things in nature were connected, from soil to humans.

Over time, supporters of sustainable agriculture began to use the word "organic" to signify that a food had been grown or raised in a natural way, without chemical fertilizers, herbicides, pesticides, hormones, or antibiotics. When meat is organic it means that byproducts from other animals were never in the livestock feed. Organic meat also means the animals it came from ate organic feed that did not contain herbicides, pesticides, hormones, or antibiotics.

Before a product can be labeled "organic," government-approved inspectors make sure the farms and farmers are following all the rules necessary to meet organic standards. Other companies that handle the food before it gets to the supermarket or restaurant must also follow the rules.

As consumer demand for organic food grew, so did the number, and size, of organic farms. With growing demand for organic foods, many large agricultural businesses, or agribusinesses, bought interests in organic farms and acquired new, organic food brands. In order to gain the business of large, chain supermarkets, the organic products had to be competitive in price. This meant that many organic farms and producers became very large in scale.

Industrial organic farming grew to make up a large portion of the organic market. These farms were larger than traditional, sustainable farms and were not as **diverse**, meaning they did not have the same variety of plants and animals together. But they still had to follow the other enforced rules to keep the "organic" label on their products. Today, organic products are the fastest-growing area of the food industry.

Conventional farming versus organic farming

The following are some basic differences between methods used by conventional farmers and those used by organic farmers:

Conventional farmers	Organic farmers
Use chemical fertilizers	Use natural fertilizers, such as manure or compost
Use pesticides	Use insects and birds, mating disruption, or traps
Use chemical herbicides	Rotate crops, till, hand weed, or mulch
Give animals antibiotics, growth hormones, and medications to prevent disease and spur higher growth levels	Give animals organic feed and allow them access to outdoors; rotate grazing schedules; offer a balanced diet and clean housing to minimize disease

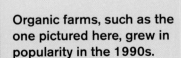

Organic farms, such as the one pictured here, grew in popularity in the 1990s.

Organic, but humane?

Until recently, when the label "organic" was on a livestock product, it did not tell a consumer anything about how the animal lived or was raised on a daily basis. For instance, organic eggs may have still been laid by hens confined to cages. As the organic portion of agriculture continued to grow, people involved in organic farming, production, and selling, as well as consumers, demanded more specific and thorough regulations to determine what foods could be labeled "organic."

In 2010 the USDA narrowed the definition of organic livestock to animals that spend one-third of the year grazing on pasture. Organic milk and meat must come from livestock that graze on pasture at least four months of the year and get 30 percent of their feed from grazing. This gives consumers more knowledge about what they are buying.

Grass-fed cattle and local farms

Another choice consumers can make involves what cattle are fed. As we have seen, livestock such as cows are not meant to eat corn, but they are often fed it because it is cheaper (see page 15). This results in the use of antibiotics and chemicals, to help the animals process the food without becoming ill. Still, this unnatural diet causes discomfort for the animals.

Because of these concerns, you will sometimes see meat in markets described by the food the animal ate. "Grass-fed," "pasture-fed," and "free-range" beef means that the steer (male beef cow) ate grass its whole life, rather than processed corn or soy (the conventional feed for cattle after six months). The steer also spends some time outdoors on pastureland—usually at least one-third of the year—during its entire lifetime.

Raising cattle on pastureland is an age-old tradition and a natural lifestyle for cattle.

Small farms can sell their produce at local farmers' markets, which are growing in popularity.

Another increasingly popular choice consumers are making it to "buy local." Farmers' markets—markets where local farmers gather on a regular basis to sell products from their farms—have become popular. Consumers can get fresh, often organic, local, in-season foods. Meats are available from local, humane farms, and are fresher since they do not travel as far as most meats in the supermarket. This gives consumers more control over knowing who farmed their food and what methods were used. Locally grown foods also use fewer fossil fuels to get to market. When you buy local, you are putting your money back into the local economy.

Case study: Brazil's grass-fed beef

Brazil is a large producer and exporter of traditionally raised, grass-fed beef. This means the cattle graze outdoors on open, grassy pasture. Since it grazes in the open, the steer (and beef) is also "free range." Europe's beef industry struggled to recover from the impact of mad cow disease (see page 14). When a single mad cow case was discovered in the United States at the end of 2003, around 70 countries banned U.S. beef. With these safety and health concerns, beef consumers looked for more natural beef. This helped Brazil, which saw its beef exports triple between 1998 and 2004.

The Future of Livestock Farming

According to the FAO, livestock farming makes up 40 percent of the total value of agriculture worldwide. It contributes 25 percent of dietary protein and 15 percent of total food energy to people globally. Livestock farming is also one of the fastest-growing parts of the agricultural economy.

Armed with this knowledge, how can we make sure livestock agriculture can continue well into the future—without harming the environment, without harming people's health, and without being unnecessarily cruel to animals? The following are some ways to go about finding **ethical** solutions:

- Smaller, diverse, sustainable farms are one answer, with a mix of livestock and crops. Getting back to the models of hundreds of years ago, these kinds of farms sustain themselves, feed local people, and do minimal damage to the environment.

- Eating food grown locally is probably the best, easiest, and biggest way to reduce our impact on the environment.

ALICE WATERS AND THE EDIBLE SCHOOLYARD

Alice Waters is the executive chef, founder, and owner of the Chez Panisse restaurant in Berkeley, California. Her philosophy of food is that cooking should be based on the freshest seasonal ingredients that are produced locally and in a sustainable way.

In 1996 Waters helped create the Edible Schoolyard, which incorporates a garden and kitchen classroom into a middle school and the school lunch program. There is a curriculum to go along with the program, and the students learn about good health, sustainable agriculture, and cooking, along with their math, science, and humanities subjects. The program inspired other school gardens and similar programs across the United States.

- Using more natural feed for animals will help avoid diseases, while reducing the need for medicines and hormones in animals' diets.

- Finally, people simply need to be prepared to pay more for meat—or to eat less of it—if they want better guarantees of healthy, safe, and humane practices in animal agriculture.

Can organic farms produce enough food for everyone?

People want safer, healthier, more natural animal products, as well as fruits and vegetables. As we have seen, organic agriculture is growing fast, along with demand. But will sustainable, organic farms still be able to produce enough food for everyone?

Research suggests that yields (amounts of crops produced) from organic farms can equal those from conventional farms. In a study done by the University of Michigan's School of Natural Resources and Environment, yields from organic and conventional farms were almost equal in developed countries. In developing countries, organic methods could increase food production significantly. Organic farms also grow a wider variety of crops and livestock. This helps reduce the chance of crop failure or low production if there is a problem with a certain crop or certain type of animal.

People need to be selective and educated consumers if they want to have healthy, ethically raised meats.

Are insects the new meat?

Livestock farming takes up a great deal of land and resources, emits greenhouse gases, and is in greater demand as the global population grows. With the world population approaching seven billion, people are considering alternative sources of meat to feed the world. One such source of meat protein is insects. The FAO is working to promote insects as food.

You may not like the idea, but eating insects for food is a common practice across most parts of the world. The most commonly eaten insects include beetles (such as ants, bees, and wasps), grasshoppers and crickets, and moths and butterflies. Insects are very nutritious, and some have as much protein as meat and fish. Some insects are also rich in fat and contain important vitamins and minerals. A serving of grasshoppers has nearly as much protein as ground beef.

Grasshoppers and other insects can be farmed more cheaply on much less land. And edible insects could provide new jobs for rural people (people who live in the countryside) who harvest and farm them. More regulations need to be in place to ensure insect food will be safe, and that they do not contain large amounts of chemicals from insecticides (chemicals used to kill insects). Then there is the matter of trying to get more squeamish people in developed countries to give insects a try. But don't be surprised if you have more exposure to edible insects in your lifetime!

Are insects coming to a plate near you?

Meat without animals?

Have you ever heard of growing meat in a laboratory? Scientists did just that at the end of 2009. Scientists in Holland used cells from a live pig to grow pork in a laboratory. They believe that their scientific breakthrough could lead to processed meat products being made from laboratory meat in as few as five years. This would mean creating living meat tissue without harming an animal.

We make the future: It's a matter of choice

Meat and other animal products are growing more popular because there are more people on the planet who can afford and want them. Humans will continue to raise livestock for food.

What sacrifices would you make, and how much would you pay, to know that you are getting safe, high-quality meat, eggs, and dairy? Or to know that your food was grown in a sustainable way? Or to know that you were not a participant in animal cruelty?

It is up to each individual to decide what part he or she will play, if any, in the livestock industry. We as consumers can send a clear message to the livestock industry depending on how we spend our money. It all comes down to choice.

What do you think?
Some questions to think about

Now that you have read this book, ask yourself the following questions:

- What do you think will need to be done in the future to make sure the people of the planet have enough food, without risking damage to the environment and to people's health?

- What could you and your family do to help make sure these things happen?

- After reading about how the livestock industry works, how do you feel about eating meat?

- How much more would you pay to know that an animal that gave you food had a good life and was treated well until it died?

Food Facts

These graphs come from FAO data showing worldwide food trends up through the year 2009. What do you think we can do to make sure that humans around the world are eating sustainably, and that everyone is getting enough to eat?

Source: FAO, 2009

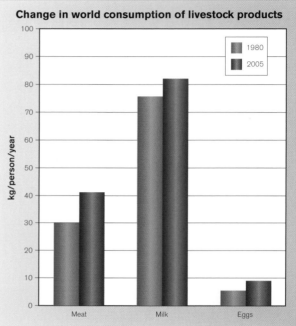

Source: FAO, 2009

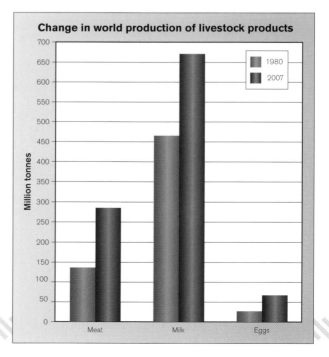

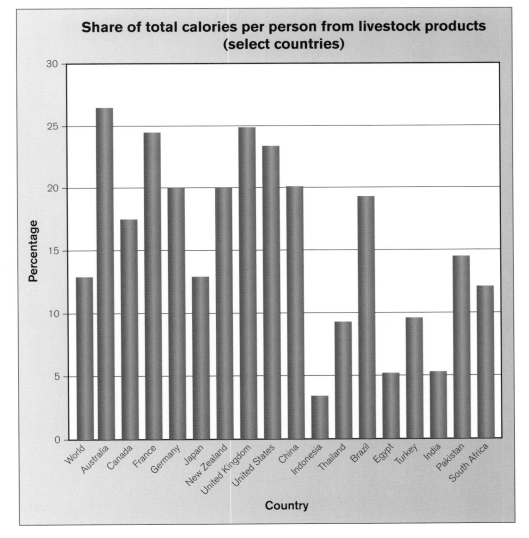

Share of total calories per person from livestock products (select countries)

Source: FAO, 2009

Glossary

antibiotic drug used to kill bacteria and prevent or cure infections

artificially inseminate medical process of making a female pregnant by using scientific equipment, rather than mating

castrate remove the testicles of a male animal

consumer someone who buys and uses something

crop rotation practice of changing the crops grown in a field each year or season in order to preserve the nutrients and quality of the soil

developed country country that is considered more advanced in its industry, technology, and economy

developing country country that is working to develop its resources and economies through industrialization and new technology

diverse different from each other

domesticated describes animals that are made able to work for people or live with them as pets

ecosystem all the plants and animals in a certain area and their relationship to each other and their environment

ethical morally good or correct

export product sold to another country; also the act of selling a product to another country

factory farm type of farm in which large numbers of animals are kept inside, in small spaces or cages, and made to grow or produce eggs or milk very quickly

feedlot area where livestock are gathered to be fed and fattened for market

fertilizer substance put on the soil to replenish its nutrients and make plants grow

fossil fuel fuel such as oil or coal produced by the gradual decaying of plants or animals over millions of years

free range relating to farming that allows animals such as chickens and pigs to move around and eat naturally outdoors, rather than being kept inside a restricted space

global warming increase in world temperatures caused by increased amounts of greenhouse gases, such as carbon dioxide, around Earth

greenhouse gas gas, such as carbon dioxide or methane, that is thought to trap heat around Earth and contribute to global warming

herbicide substance used to kill unwanted plants

hormone chemical substance produced by the body that affects its growth, development, and health

humane treating a living thing in a way that is not cruel and causes it as little suffering as possible

incubate act of keeping eggs warm until they hatch

industrialized having a lot of factories and modern production

intensive farming that produces a lot of food from a small amount of land

manure waste matter from animals

organic relating to methods of growing food without using artificial chemicals; also describing food grown in this way

overgrazing when animals graze too much in one spot, such that the edible grasses do not have time to grow back and recover

pesticide chemical substance used to kill insects and other animals that destroy crops

poultry birds such as chickens, turkeys, and ducks that are kept on farms in order to produce meat and eggs

process preserve or improve something to make it ready to be used or sold

ruminant animal such as a cow that has several stomachs and eats grass

selective breeding intentional mating of two animals in order to produce offspring with certain characteristics

species group of plants or animals whose members are similar and can mate to produce young

sustainable something that is able to continue each year without causing damage to the environment

trough long, narrow, open container that holds food or water for farm animals

unethical morally wrong

urban relating to towns and cities

wean when a baby or young animal is slowly stopped from feeding on its mother's milk and given different food instead

Further Information

Books

Baines, John D. *Food and Farming* (*Global Village* series). Mankato, MN: Smart Apple Media, 2009.

Baur, Gene. *Farm Sanctuary: Changing Hearts and Minds About Animals and Food.* New York, NY: Touchstone, 2008.

Chevat, Richie, and Michael Pollan. *The Omnivore's Dilemma: The Secrets Behind What You Eat.* New York, NY: Dial, 2009.

Egendorf, Laura K. *Food* (*Opposing Viewpoints* series). Detroit, MI: Greenhaven, 2006.

Eisnitz, Gail A. *Slaughterhouse: The Shocking Story of Greed, Neglect, and Inhumane Treatment Inside the U.S. Meat Industry.* Amherst, MA: Prometheus, 2007.

Pollan, Michael. *Food Rules: An Eater's Manual.* New York, NY: Penguin, 2009.

Schlosser, Eric, and Charles Wilson. *Chew on This: Everything You Don't Want to Know About Fast Food.* Boston, MA: Houghton Mifflin, 2007.

Sherrow, Victoria, and Alan Marzilli. *Food Safety* (*Point/Counterpoint* series). New York, NY: Chelsea House, 2008.

Weber, Karl. *Food, Inc.* New York, NY: PublicAffairs, 2009.

DVDs

Food, Inc. Los Angeles, CA: Magnolia Home Entertainment, 2009.

Foodmatters. Metuchen, NJ: Passion River Films, 2009.

The Future of Food. Mill Valley, CA: Lily, 2004.

King Corn. New York, NY: Docurama, 2008.

Our Daily Bread. Brooklyn, NY: Icarus Films, 2006.

Websites

www.fao.org
At the official website of the Food and Agriculture Organization of the United Nations (FAO), you can find a lot of global information about food and agriculture, including links to international statistics and publications relating to agricultural issues worldwide.

www.who.int/nutrition/en
This website of the World Health Organization (WHO) discusses nutrition and health and offers useful links for further research.

www.epa.gov/agriculture/index.html
This website of the U.S. Environmental Protection Agency (EPA) offers information and links relating to agriculture and its impact on the environment.

www.humanesociety.org/animals/browse_animals.html
At the website of the Humane Society of the United States you will find a link to "Farm Animals," where you will find information and videos concerning specific farm animals and how they are treated.

www.fda.gov
The website of the U.S. Food and Drug Administration (FDA) offers information about public health and the nation's food supply.

Topics for further research

Research the various organizations that promote animal rights, their goals, and their arguments. Which one do you agree or disagree with?

What does the latest medical research say about hormones used in raising beef cattle? What are the good and bad reasons to use them?

What is the difference between industrial organic farming and traditional farming? What are the advantages and disadvantages of both?

What kinds of insects are eaten as food around the world? What are the health reasons for and against eating insects?

What are the reasons for and against vegetarianism? What about health? Cost? Ethics?

Where did domestic livestock animals originally come from? What were their wild ancestors like compared to the domesticated versions found today? Could farm animals survive in the wild today?

What is bird flu and what causes it? What are the risks with livestock farming when it comes to human health and disease?

Index